THE SINGULAR CAT

THE SINGULAR CAT

Photographs by JANE BOWN

Introduction by Julie Welch

BLOOMSBURY

For Granny Gosling, who rescued Tom in a blizzard

First published 1988

Copyright © 1988 by Jane Bown

Bloomsbury Publishing Limited, 2 Soho Square, London W1V 5DE

British Library Cataloguing in Publication data

Bown, Jane
   The Singular Cat
   1. Pets: Cats – Illustrated
   1. Title
   636.8'7

ISBN 0-7475-0307-9

Many thanks to David Watkinson of *The Observer* and
Mike Spry of Downtown Darkroom for their care and
patience in printing the photographs.
Designed by Anita Plank
**Printed and bound in Great Britain by BAS Printers Ltd
Over Wallop, Stockbridge, Hampshire**

Contents

Introduction

These are cats which Jane has photographed over the years. Some she discovered on journeys, others at work, some just rolled up at her house. She photographs cats because she likes them. I am sure the compliment is reciprocated because cats won't just pose for anyone. If they don't like the look of your hat they will nip off sharpish behind the sofa and it takes four men and a block and tackle to get them out.

Jane Bown in action often seems rather feline herself – quiet, watchful, waiting for the right image, the right moment, like a British Blue serenely assessing the contents of the goldfish pond. From time to time it has been my privilege to work with her on newspaper assignments and she has always been the least obtrusive, most observant and kindly of photographers. I love her humour and humaneness, her empathy with her subjects, her gravitas and gentleness, the fact that she has never taken a commonplace picture. Everything seems to be lit from the inside.

I am convinced that cats know they are being photographed, even encourage the photographer to seek them out. All those positions they adopt – the hearthrug sprawl, the hind-leg-in-the-air ablutions, the rugby ball when they tuck all four legs underneath them to form a perfect perching oval. Always looking for the pattern that the sunlight makes on the carpet, the stripes on the counterpane, the hexagon of wire netting that fits like a monocle round one beady feline eye. As Jane says, if they see you cutting up any material they come and sit on it. Chase non-existent mice in fallen leaves. Ponder the meaning of life high up in a plane tree, knowing the lens is on them.

There are cat verbs, too. Cats lean, lounge, scavenge, scrounge, loll, roll, dabble, yowl, leap, pounce, prowl and streak. Sometimes all at once.

Jane and I did a story about cats in winter 1977. The National Cat Club's 81st Championship Show at Olympia. Jane came away with a lot of beautiful photos, some of which are in this book. I came away with a lot of cats. Archie, Poppy, Cathy and Scarlett. Archie was a red Burmese, sold to me by a nice lady judge. He was an eventful cat to own. I still dine *out on some of his antics; how he*

* *sat on the VAT inspector's head*
* *retrieved socks if you threw them for him*
* *broke his leg by falling off a one-foot-high bench*
* *habitually cramponned up the woodchip-papered dining room walls*
* *ate half the leg of pork earmarked for that night's dinner party for a famous lady TV presenter (the other half cooked up fine once I'd trimmed off the chewed bits).*

Archie was the leader of my pack of cats who also included hairy ginger Mildred who thought she was Elizabeth Taylor when actually she looked like an old rug. Also Zelda and Sheba, Cathy's two mysterious daughters, and her son Arthur who did not have a first-rate mind but was a valiant creature who survived three weeks imprisonment without food or water when accidentally shut in an empty house. Also Poppy's son Tigerpaws Redsox, a redpoint Siamese, Open Class winner at the 1979 Southern Counties show, who had china blue eyes and a terrible tendency to pee in people's handbags. In those days when I was alone they all slept on my bed, a beautiful, living, loving, purring, many-coloured counterpane.

Around that time I had a friend who wrote books with titles like 'Egyptian Magic Made Simple' and 'A Boy Scout's Guide to Runes'. She believed that cats were space creatures, evolved descendants of pilgrims from a distant undiscovered planet, the name of which now eludes my memory. She was adamant; there were no cats in heaven. We fell out over this. Of course there are cats in heaven – but no need to empty litter trays.

I lived in a little terrace house in Wandsworth, where Archie remained with its new owner after I left it to get married. (He had taken against my husband's two cats and every time he caught sight of them would do a convincing impersonation of a heat-seeking missile.) I miss him dreadfully, though the wallpaper is in better nick.

At Jane's house, there are obviously lots of interesting alcoves, cran-

12

nies, cupboards, boxes, etc. for the cats to have kittens in. Cats are always so intrepid when giving birth, unlike us craven humans. Ledges, tallboys, hedgerows, piles of old newspapers, the new kingsize bed from Harrods with its white lace duvet cover and special antique cushions from a little shop in the Fulham Road. Poppy had Redsox under the dining room table, swaddling him in the Laura Ashley tablecloth.

My favourite among this collection of Jane's is the picture of Mr Tom Gosling in the cardboard box. It is quite extraordinary the lure that cardboard boxes have for cats. Some jump inside and go fifteen rounds with them, the winner to be decided by two falls or a submission. The cardboard box always seems to win. But Mr Tom Gosling is obviously imagining himself at the controls of some great flying machine. Perhaps he is returning to the land of his ancestors, that far-off planet the name of which now eludes me.

Mr Tom Gosling is a great big black monster of unknown age who appeared one day on Granny Gosling's doorstep in Wales. He came out of a blizzard like yonder page in Good King Wenceslas. She took him in and gave him her love and her lap until she died. A born survivor, he came home with Jane in a cardboard box. In colour he is a very dense black flecked with grey, as though bits of the blizzard stuck to him indelibly.

Ah, cat colours. Soot and lead and raisin black, stripey tabbies with starched white shirtfronts, tortoiseshells the pattern of the horn-rimmed specs you used to get on the National Health. Poppy, my Siamese queen, was what you called a tortiepoint if you bred Siamese. If you didn't breed Siamese, I can only liken her colour to fog on the M1.

I remember bringing Poppy home as a kitten. Freddy, my firstborn son, was nine at the time. Poppy seemed mainly to be made of ears, but enormously confident. She would stare at you adoringly out of her large blue eyes, the eye dance that mothers perform with their babies. A big, peace-loving, sane Siamese with a staccato bark of a voice. She died last year, having been with me through a divorce, a marriage, two houses, two *more babies, Freddy now grown to be a man.*

The whitish, rather pretty kitten in this book is Queenie. The late Queenie – that picture was taken 25 years ago. Jane's first cat. She lived to a very good age and then got a bad ear. She was one of those cats who, to register utter disapproval, would turn her back. Now Jane has four cats. The two Head Cats have both had many families. The disaster area is in black-and-white cats. They've all been run over. Even Tombola, son of Trilby, sibling of Tam O'Shanter. Tombola's original name was Bowler. The entire litter was named after hats. They were not called kittens, but millinery. Trilby bore them on the top shelf of the china cupboard. Jane gets very involved with her cats, particularly the matriarchs. Trilby is 14, one-eyed, very huffy at the time of writing, won't jump on the bed, will only lurk around the fireside. When you pick her up she is as light as a falling leaf.

Jane's cats are very clever at finding which bed to sleep on during the day. Musical chairs, they play. Jane says that once you've owned a cat you are hooked for ever and I think this is true.

Julie Welch

Cats

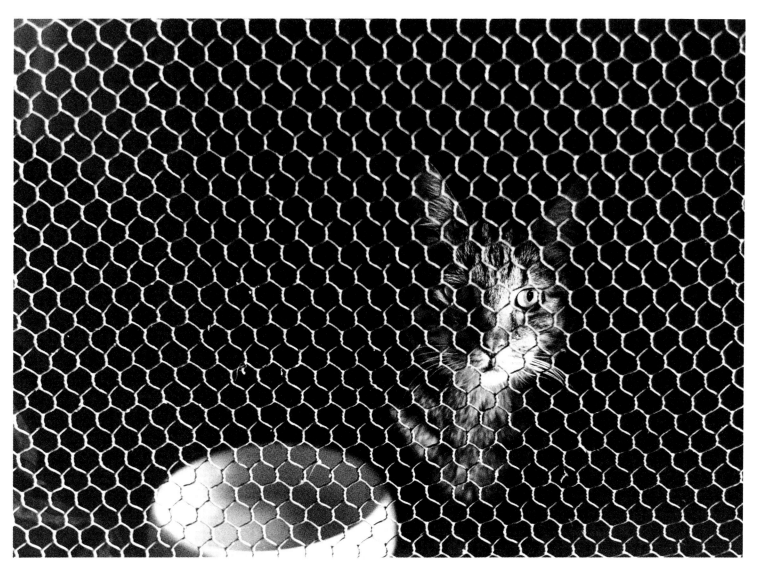

Cat in quarantine

18

Stray cat in Fitzroy Square, London

Another Fitzroy Square resident

20

Italian cats

Village cat near Naples

Cat encountered on an assignment with Julie Welch

24

Alley cat in Shanghai

Performing cat in La Rochelle

Wild cats at Fulham Broadway, London

Scavenging outside the station

Torn-eared veterans in Dorset

Mews-dwelling cat, London

Reclining cats in Soho, London

Barn cat

34

Lone cat in the fish market at Milford Haven docks

35

Cat group, Milford Haven docks

Venetian cats

38

Station cat at King's Cross, London

39

Thames barge cat, London

On the quay at Cawsand, Devon

Hotel cat in Tenby, Wales

43

Cat in a tree, Hereford

Show cat in travelling basket

Cat in the window, Rome

Cat in the window, Positano

Show cat on show

Show cat in waiting

A matching pair of show cats

Welsh farm cats, near Llandeilo

Italian village kitten among mountain ruins

Pavement cat in Hackney

55

Moppet in a tree, Sevenoaks, Kent

David Knopfler's musical kitten

Julian Trevelyan's studio cat

58

Laughing cat, Italy

59

Solemn cat staring

Shop window slumbers, Wellington, Somerset

Tom Gosling and friends

63

Queenie – the first of a long line, in pre-motherhood days

Queenie and Dusty – rough justice between cat and her kitten

Queenie and Dusty – another litter followed Dusty and siblings

Contentment...

The lazy days of summer

Ginge puss – a terrible old stray who never acquired a proper name

Ginge puss – attempting a more elegant pose

Trilby – Queenie's successor, the five-shilling cat

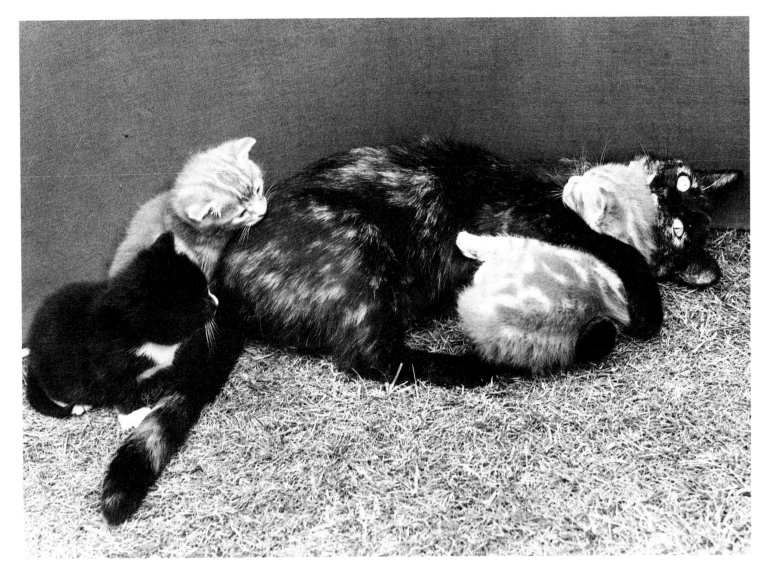

Trilby with kittens
Spats and Tammy, who stayed, and Fez, who found a home in another branch of the family

Fez and Spats – an early alliance

76

Tammy...

and Spats on their look-out post

Busby – the semi-wild cat with the fox's plume, who came to stay

Tombola – a new addition to the ranks

Tombola playing

Gandalf and Merlin – visiting cousins, looking out

83

Tombola and Tammy – home cats looking in

Tammy – in a good light

Tammy and Tombola – kitchen antics

Tom Gosling – an unexpected acquisition, arriving in a cardboard box

Tombola meets Tom Gosling – a wary sizing-up

Tombola, Tom Gosling and Tammy – a place for everyone

90

Tom Gosling – warily emerging from a window

Trilby – the matriarch in old age, now with only one eye

Tammy and friend